OCT   2008

The new Solar System
Mars

Robin Birch

CHELSEA CLUBHOUSE
An Imprint of Chelsea House Publishers

This edition published in 2008 in the United States of America by Chelsea Clubhouse, a division of Chelsea House Publishers.

Chelsea Clubhouse
An imprint of Chelsea House Publishers
132 West 31st Street
New York, NY 10001

Chelsea Clubhouse books are available at special discounts when purchased in bulk quantities for businesses, associations, institutions, or sales promotions. Please call our Special Sales Department in New York at (212) 967-8800 or (800) 322-8755.

You can find Chelsea Clubhouse on the World Wide Web at: http://www.chelseahouse.com

First published in 2004 by
MACMILLAN EDUCATION AUSTRALIA PTY LTD
15–19 Claremont Street, South Yarra, 3141

Visit our Web site at www.macmillan.com.au or go directly to www.macmillanlibrary.com.au

Associated companies and representatives throughout the world.

Library of Congress Cataloging-in-Publication Data

Birch, Robin.
    Mars / Robin Birch. — Second ed.
    p. cm. — (The new solar system)
    Includes index.
    ISBN 978-1-60413-211-3
    1. Mars (Planet) —Juvenile literature. I. Title.
    QB641.B495 2008
    523.43—dc22

                                    2007051545

Edited by Anna Fern
Text and cover design by Cristina Neri, Canary Graphic Design
Photo research by Legend Images
Illustrations by Melissa Webb, Noisypics

Printed in the United States of America

Acknowledgements

The author and publisher are grateful to the following for permission to reproduce copyright material:

Cover photograph of Mars courtesy of Reuters.

Art Archive, p. 5 (left); JPL/TSADO/Tom Stack/Auscape, p. 25 (top); Digital Vision, pp. 5 (right), 27; Calvin J. Hamilton, pp. 7, 11, 13 (bottom), 16, 18, 23, 24, 25 (bottom); Medialab, ESA 2001, p. 12; Walter Myers/www.arcadiastreet.com, p. 10; NASA/GRIN, p. 15; NASA/Human Space Flight, p. 29; NASA/JPL/MSSS, pp. 13 (top), 14; NASA/NSSDC, p. 26; NASA/Planetary Photojournal, p. 28; NASA/US Geological Survey, p. 19; Photolibrary.com/SPL, pp. 4 (bottom right), 6, 17, 20, 21, 22.

Background and border images, including view of Mars, courtesy of Photodisc.

While every care has been taken to trace and acknowledge copyright, the publisher offers their apologies for any accidental infringement where copyright has proved untraceable. Where the attempt has been unsuccessful, the publisher welcomes information that would redress the situation.

Please note
At the time of printing, the Internet addresses appearing in this book were correct. Owing to the dynamic nature of the Internet, however, we cannot guarantee that all these addresses will remain correct.

Contents

Glossary words

When you see a word printed in bold, **like this**, you can look up its meaning in the glossary on page 31.

Discovering Mars

The **planet** Mars looks like an orange **star** in the sky. The rocks on Mars are a red-brown color and it is known as "the red planet."

Mars may be in the sky at any time of night. Sometimes it is very bright. At other times it is no brighter than many stars in the sky.

▲ This is the symbol for Mars.

Mars

▲ Mars in the night sky

The word "planet" means "wanderer." Stars always make the same pattern in the sky. Planets change their location in the sky, compared to the stars around them. This is why they were called "wanderers."

Mars was named after Mars, the Roman god of war. The planet Mars was probably given this name because its orange-red color is the color of blood and war.

▼ The planet Mars

▲ The Roman god Mars

A few details of Mars can be seen from Earth, through a **telescope**. Some **astronomers** who looked at Mars about 100 years ago through telescopes saw patterns on Mars. They thought living things similar to humans had made the patterns.

Mars was first visited by the **space probe** *Mariner 4* in 1965. *Mariner 4*'s close-up photographs of Mars showed **craters**, but no signs of life. In 1976, the space probes *Viking 1* and *Viking 2* started taking excellent pictures of Mars's surface, and began beaming them back to Earth.

The Fourth Planet

The planet Mars **revolves** around the Sun, along with seven other planets and many other bodies. The Sun, planets, and other bodies together are called the solar system. Mars is the fourth planet from the Sun.

There are eight planets in the solar system. Mercury, Venus, Earth, and Mars are made of rock. They are the smallest planets, and are closest to the Sun. Jupiter, Saturn, Uranus, and Neptune are made mainly of **gas** and liquid. They are the largest planets, and are farthest from the Sun.

The solar system also has dwarf planets. The first three bodies to be called dwarf planets were Ceres, Pluto, and Eris. Ceres is an asteroid. Pluto and Eris are known as **trans-Neptunian objects**.

A planet is a body that:

- orbits the Sun
- is nearly round in shape
- has cleared the area around its orbit (its **gravity** is strong enough)

A dwarf planet is a body that:

- orbits the Sun
- is nearly round in shape
- has not cleared the area around its orbit
- is not a **moon**

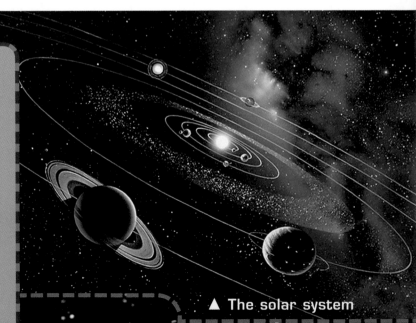
▲ The solar system

6

There are also many small solar system bodies in the solar system. These include asteroids, comets, trans-Neptunian objects, and other small bodies which have not been called dwarf planets.

Asteroids are made of rock. Most of them, including dwarf planet Ceres, orbit the Sun in a path called the asteroid belt. The asteroid belt lies between the orbits of Mars and Jupiter. Comets are made mainly of ice and rock. When their orbits bring them close to the Sun, comets grow a tail. Trans-Neptunian objects are icy, and orbit the Sun farther out on average than Neptune.

▶ The eight planets are Mercury, Venus, Earth, Mars, Jupiter, Saturn, Uranus, and Neptune.

The solar system is about 4,600 million years old.

Planet	Average distance from Sun	
Mercury	35,960,000 miles	(57,910,000 kilometers)
Venus	67,190,000 miles	(108,200,000 kilometers)
Earth	92,900,000 miles	(149,600,000 kilometers)
Mars	141,550,000 miles	(227,940,000 kilometers)
Jupiter	483,340,000 miles	(778,330,000 kilometers)
Saturn	887,660,000 miles	(1,429,400,000 kilometers)
Uranus	1,782,880,000 miles	(2,870,990,000 kilometers)
Neptune	2,796,000,000 miles	(4,504,000,000 kilometers)

The name "solar system" comes from the word "Sol," the Latin name for the Sun.

On Mars

As it travels around the Sun, the rocky planet Mars spins on its **axis**.

Rotation and Revolution

Mars **rotates** on its axis every 24.62 Earth hours. This means that a day on Mars is about the same length as a day on Earth. Mars's axis is tilted at an angle of 25 degrees, which is similar to the tilt of Earth's axis.

It takes 687 Earth days for Mars to revolve around the Sun once. This is the length of Mars's year—nearly twice as long as an Earth year. The Sun's gravity keeps Mars revolving around it.

The orbit of Mars around the Sun is elliptical, or oval-shaped. When Mars comes closer to the Sun, it becomes hotter. When Mars is farther from the Sun, it becomes colder.

Sun

Axis

Day

Night

▲ Mars rotates on its axis as it revolves around the Sun.

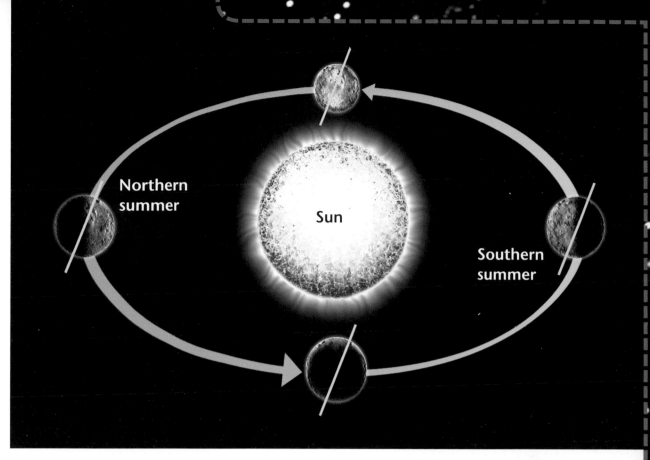

Northern summer

Sun

Southern summer

▲ Seasons on Mars

Seasons

Because Mars's axis is tilted, Mars has seasons, the same as Earth. When Mars's northern **hemisphere** is tilted towards the Sun, it is summer in the northern hemisphere and winter in the southern hemisphere. Half a Mars year later, the southern hemisphere is tilted towards the Sun. Then it is summer in the southern hemisphere and winter in the northern hemisphere.

The temperature on Mars reaches up to 81 degrees Fahrenheit (27 degrees Celsius) in summer and goes down to –207 degrees Fahrenheit (–133 degrees Celsius) in winter. Each of Mars's four seasons lasts for six months, because Mars's year is two Earth years long.

Size and Structure

Mars is 4,219 miles (6,794 kilometers) in **diameter**. It is smaller than Earth. Mars is most likely made up of a **core**, a **mantle**, and a **crust**.

The core of Mars would be very **dense** and would probably be about 2,100 miles (3,400 kilometers) in diameter. It is probably made of **molten** iron mixed with large amounts of the substance sulfur.

Mars probably has a wide mantle around the core made of hot, molten rock. The crust on the outside is probably 20 to 50 miles (35 to 80 kilometers) thick.

▼ Compare the size of Mars (right) and Earth (left).

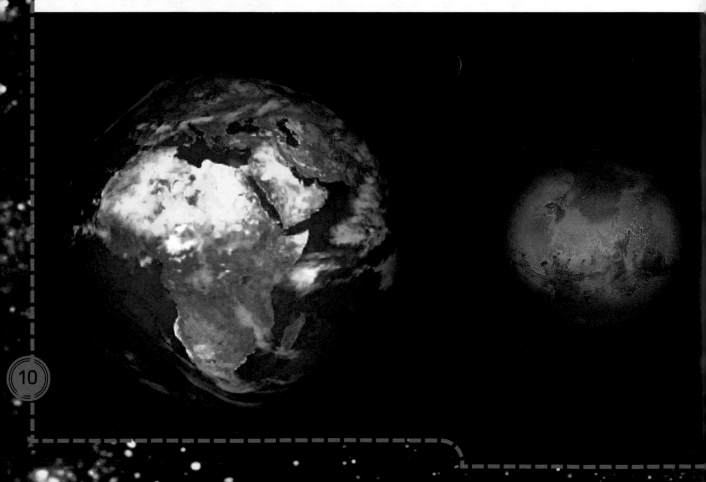

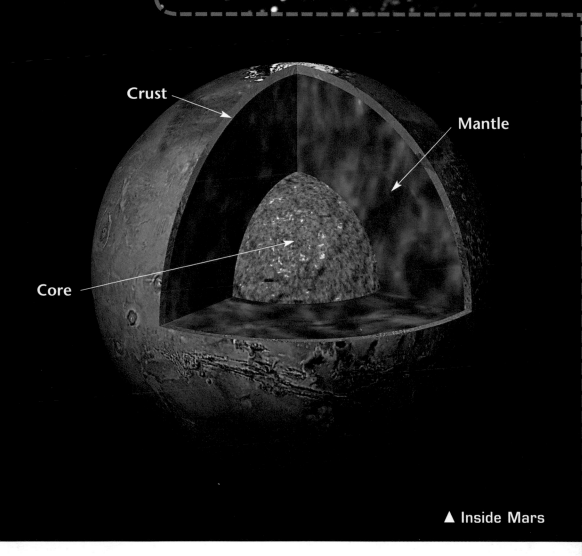

▲ Inside Mars

Crust • Mantle • Core

Crust

Mars's crust appears not to move around or fold up to make mountains and ridges like Earth's crust. The crust on Mars does have weak spots in it. **Volcanoes** have formed in these places, because **lava** has come though the crust to the surface. The lava has come from the mantle, below the crust.

The crust of Mars has a large amount of iron in it. The iron has gone rusty from being exposed to the substance oxygen a long time ago. This gives Mars its red color.

Atmosphere

Mars has a very thin **atmosphere**, made mostly of carbon dioxide gas. There is almost no water in the atmosphere. The sky on Mars is normally a clear, pale-pink color, caused by red dust in the atmosphere.

Mars sometimes has strong winds in its atmosphere which can blow at up to 120 miles (200 kilometers) per hour. The winds make huge dust storms which sometimes cover the whole planet. They can last for weeks. The dust storms turn the sky dark orange-pink.

▲ Dust storm on Mars

The thin atmosphere of Mars holds some heat from the Sun. It acts like a blanket, keeping the planet warm. However, Mars is not kept as warm as the planets Venus and Earth are by their thick atmospheres.

Clouds

Mars does not have very many clouds, compared to the other planets which have atmospheres. This is why it is possible to take good photographs of Mars, showing many details of the surface. It is mainly dust storms that get in the way of sceing details on Mars.

▲ Mars has a few clouds

▼ Clouds in a valley on Mars

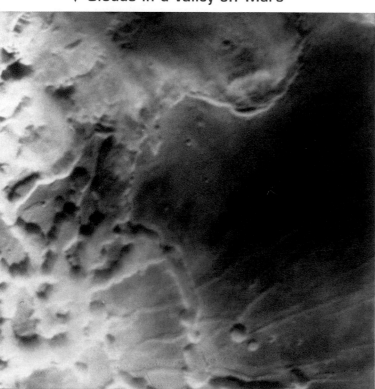

Mars has some clouds from time to time. They are made of tiny **crystals** of water ice and carbon dioxide ice. The clouds are usually found high up in the atmosphere. They can also be found swirling around the slopes of volcanoes. Valleys and canyons on Mars can have fog in them, early in the morning.

13

Ice caps

Mars has ice caps on its north and south **poles**. They look similar to the ice caps on the North and South poles of Earth. The ice caps on Mars are made mainly of solid carbon dioxide. This is also called carbon dioxide ice or "dry ice."

Carbon dioxide ice turns into gas when there is some warmth. When it is summer at a pole on Mars, the ice cap there shrinks. This is because the carbon dioxide turns into gas and goes into the atmosphere. When it is winter at a pole on Mars, the ice cap grows again because carbon dioxide in the atmosphere freezes and falls to the ground.

▼ An ice cap on Mars

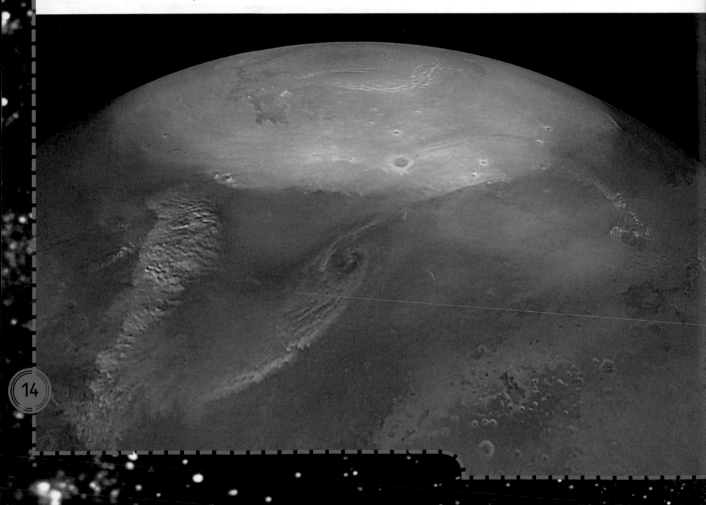

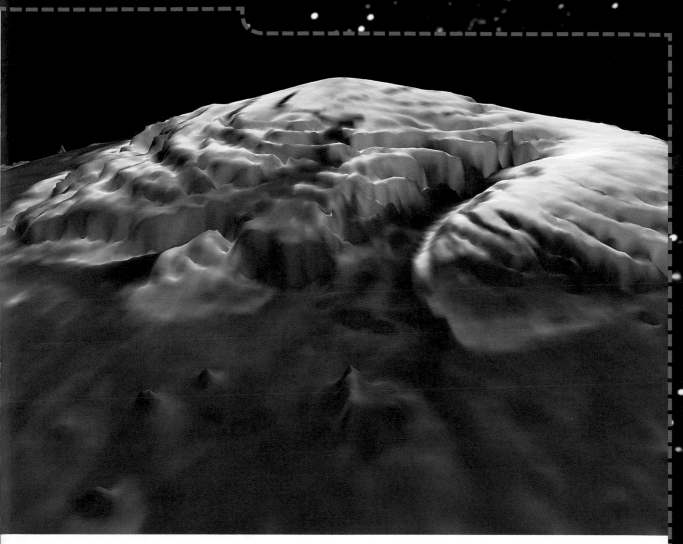

▲ Close-up of an ice cap on Mars

Mars's ice caps have layers in them. The layers are mostly carbon dioxide ice and dark-colored dust. Both ice caps have water ice (frozen water) in them.

When it is summer in the north, the carbon dioxide ice warms up and becomes a gas, leaving the water ice behind. During southern summer, the carbon dioxide ice at the south pole does not all turn into gas. We know there is water underneath because the *Mars Express* space probe has detected it.

Surface

Mars has reddish-brown, rocky ground. The surface of Mars is varied, with smooth plains, highlands, craters, canyons, valleys, and volcanoes that are probably **extinct**.

The southern hemisphere of Mars is mainly highlands. The highlands are very old and have a lot of impact craters on them which were made by asteroids hitting Mars a long time ago. The highlands look similar to the surface of Earth's Moon.

▲ The huge Hellas impact crater on Mars's southern hemisphere, in false color. It is 6 miles (9 kilometers) deep and 1,300 miles (2,100 kilometers) across.

Most of the northern hemisphere is low plains. The plains are fairly smooth, and younger than the highlands. There is a thick layer of dust covering the low northern plains. There is a definite border between the southern highlands and the low northern plains.

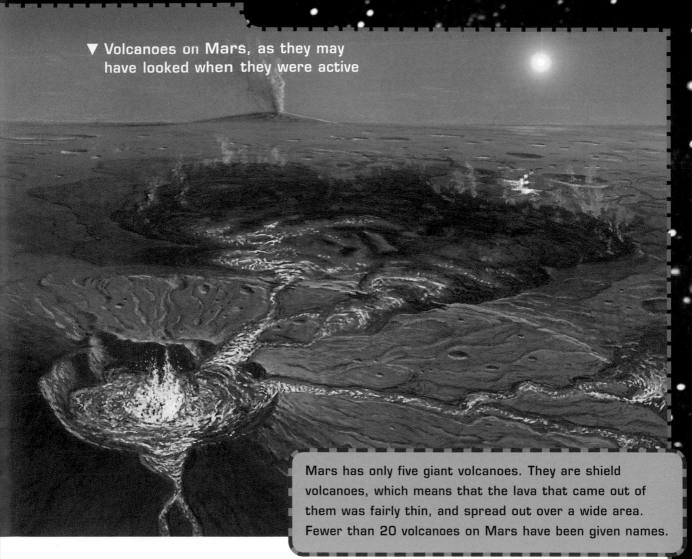

Mars has only five giant volcanoes. They are shield volcanoes, which means that the lava that came out of them was fairly thin, and spread out over a wide area. Fewer than 20 volcanoes on Mars have been given names.

Volcanoes

Mars has volcanoes, but there are not many of them. Astronomers believe the volcanoes are probably all extinct. Volcanoes are the only mountains on Mars, and there are no long mountain ranges.

One part of Mars has volcanoes which are so large they make a bulge in the shape of the planet. This area is called the Tharsis region. Its bulge is 2,500 miles (4,000 kilometers) across and 6 miles (10 kilometers) high. The biggest volcano in the Tharsis region is Olympus Mons.

Olympus Mons

Olympus Mons is the largest volcano on Mars, and the largest volcano on any planet. It is 386 miles (624 kilometers) across and 16 miles (25 kilometers) high. Olympus Mons is on the Tharsis region of Mars, near the **equator**. It is not active now.

Olympus Mons has a large, bowl-shaped hollow at the center, 50 miles (80 kilometers) across. It has several circular craters inside it, caused by collapses of lava. There is a tall cliff making a wall which goes right around the outside of Olympus Mons.

▼ Olympus Mons

Olympus Mons is a shield volcano. This makes it a wide volcano rather than a narrow one.

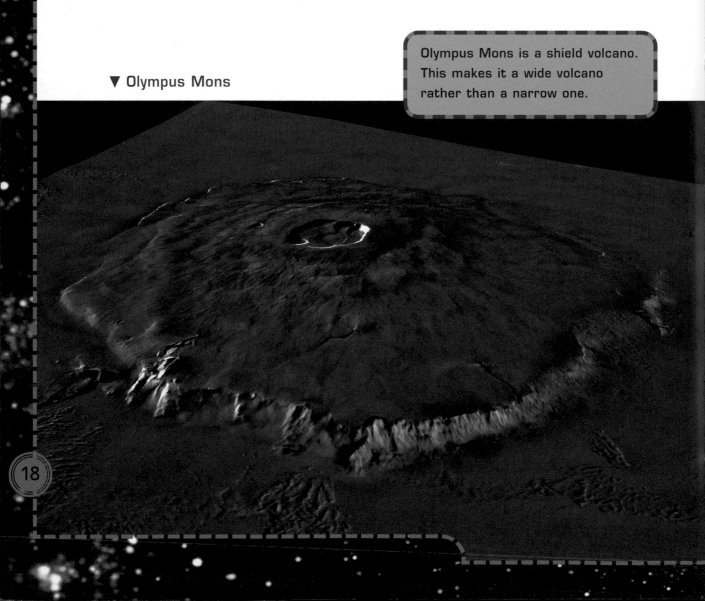

Vallis Marineris

Mars has a group of huge canyons, called Vallis Marineris, which run around part of the equator. Vallis Marineris is more than 2,500 miles (4,000 kilometers) long and up to 120 miles (200 kilometers) wide. Some parts are 4 miles (7 kilometers) deep.

Vallis Marineris was not formed by running water, but by stretching and cracking of the crust of Mars. This happened as the Tharsis bulge was being created. The Tharsis region is at the western end of Vallis Marineris.

There are many very old river channels running north across Mars, from the central part of Vallis Marineris. They run up towards the north pole.

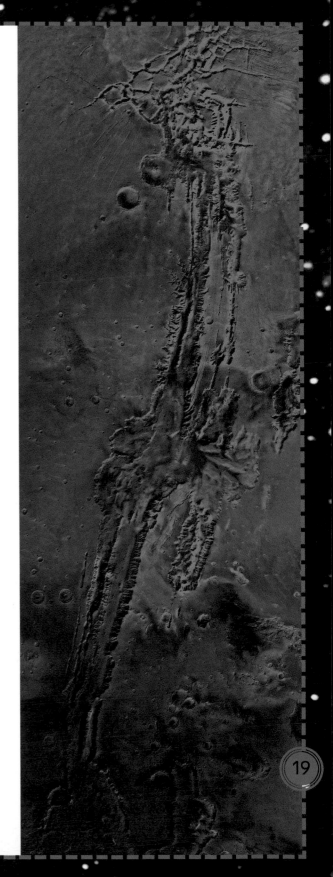

▶ Vallis Marineris

Water on Mars

Today Mars is very dry. There does not appear to be any liquid water on its surface, although some markings could be caused by water trickles. Mars probably cannot have liquid water on it because it is too cold, and the atmosphere is too thin.

On Mars, there is a small amount of frozen water in at least one of the ice caps. There is also a very small amount of water in the atmosphere, and a few clouds with water ice crystals in them.

Mars looks like it had a lot of water on it a long time ago, between 3,000 and 4,500 million years ago. The water probably did not last for very long.

▶ Empty water channels on Mars

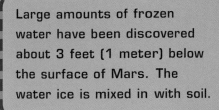

Large amounts of frozen water have been discovered about 3 feet (1 meter) below the surface of Mars. The water ice is mixed in with soil.

▶ This area on Mars may have been shaped by a flood.

Many features on Mars have been shaped by flowing water. Mars has smooth flood plains, where large amounts of water have flowed across quickly. It has hills shaped by water flowing around them, as though they were islands during a flood. Mars may have had lakes and seas. There are old, empty channels and riverbeds which look like they drained water away from floods.

Mars has rocks which are made of smaller pebbles stuck together. This type of rock has formed at the bottom of water.

Life on Mars

People have been wondering for a long time if there are living things on Mars. For living things to exist, there needs to be liquid water. It appears that Mars had liquid water on it a long time ago, which means that life could possibly have existed on Mars. If there is liquid water on Mars today, it is possible there are living organisms on Mars today.

In the 1970s, the Viking space probes did experiments on Mars to look for life. The experiments showed there was probably no life on Mars.

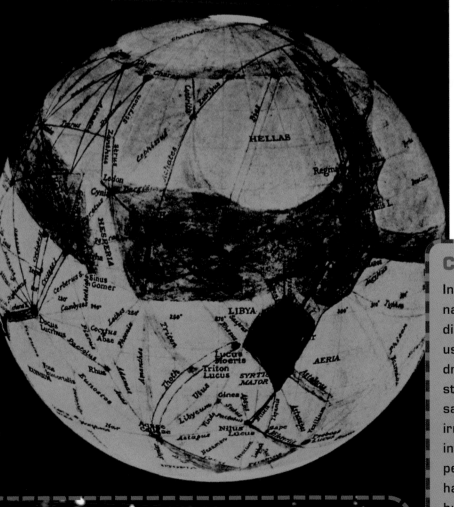

◀ Lowell's drawing of canals on Mars

Canals on Mars?

In 1906, an astronomer named Percival Lowell did drawings of Mars using a telescope. The drawings showed lots of straight lines. Lowell said the lines could be irrigation canals, built by intelligent beings. Many people believed Mars had beings similar to humans living on it.

▲ Scientists think they may have found
signs of life in this meteorite.

Microbes

Scientists have studied rocks from Mars which have landed
on Earth. These rocks were broken off Mars a long time ago
by asteroids crashing into Mars. The rocks landed on Earth
as meteorites.

One meteorite had tiny tube shapes in it which could only
be seen with a powerful microscope. The tube shapes looked
like they could have been left behind by living microorganisms.
Some scientists thought they may possibly have found signs of
life on Mars. Others thought the tube shapes were not caused
by living things.

Moons

Mars has two small **moons** called Phobos and Deimos. Both moons are probably made of rock and ice. They both have **irregular** shapes and are covered in craters.

Phobos

Phobos, the larger moon, is about 14 miles (22 kilometers) across. Phobos is closer to its planet than any other moon in the solar system. Its orbit is only 3,700 miles (6,000 kilometers) above the surface of Mars. This is so low that Phobos would not be seen from everywhere on Mars. Phobos revolves around Mars once every 7 hours and 40 minutes. It is covered with fine dust about 3 feet (1 meter) thick.

Phobos has a huge crater on it named Stickney. The crater was made when an asteroid crashed into Phobos. The crash would have nearly shattered Phobos.

▶ Phobos

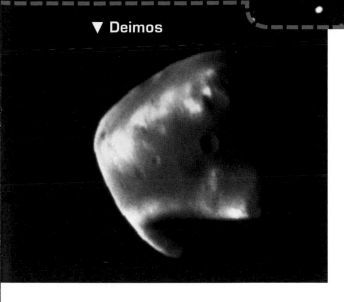

▼ Deimos

Phobos rises in the west and sets in the east. It usually rises twice in a Mars day. Phobos is slowly getting closer to Mars. In about 50 million years it will probably crash into Mars, or it may break up and make a ring of particles around Mars.

Deimos

Deimos, the smaller of Mars's two moons, is about 8 miles (13 kilometers) across. It is the smallest known moon in the solar system. Deimos orbits Mars about once every 30 hours. The orbit of Deimos is 12,000 miles (20,000 kilometers) above Mars's surface. Deimos has craters on it from being hit by asteroids, but it has a smoother surface than Phobos.

► Mars and its two moons

Exploring Mars

The first space probe to visit Mars was *Mariner 4*, in 1965. Since then, several other space probes have been sent to Mars.

Mariner 4 took close-up photos which showed Mars's craters. Information collected by *Mariner 4* helped show that the atmosphere of Mars is made of carbon dioxide.

The first space probe to land on Mars was *Mars 2*, in 1971. The space probes *Viking 1* and *Viking 2* landed on Mars in 1976 and sent a lot of information back to Earth for several years. They made pictures of Mars's surface showing the landscape, and observed Mars's weather.

Each *Viking* consisted of a lander and an orbiter. The landers landed on Mars. The orbiters orbited Mars and made detailed maps of the planet.

▶ This picture of the landscape on Mars was taken by the *Viking* mission.

When *Mars Pathfinder* landed on Mars, it bounced up 50 feet (15 meters). It bounced 15 more times, rolled, and landed half a mile (1 kilometer) away.

► An artist's impression of *Sojourner* on Mars. The *Mars Pathfinder* vehicle can be seen in the background.

Mars Pathfinder

The space probe *Mars Pathfinder* landed on Mars in 1997. *Mars Pathfinder* consisted of a lander and a surface rover. The lander landed in the northern hemisphere of Mars, in the Ares Vallis region. The surface rover, named *Sojourner*, rolled out of the lander two days later. *Sojourner* was a small robot with six wheels.

Sojourner moved around on the ground of Mars. It was controlled by people on Earth. *Sojourner* took 550 pictures of Mars, and the lander took more than 16,000 pictures of Mars. *Mars Pathfinder* also studied rocks to see what they were made of, and gathered information about the weather. It sent information back to Earth for 83 days.

More missions

Mars Odyssey was sent to Mars in 2001. It has discovered large amounts of hydrogen in the upper layer of Mars's soil, suggesting there is water on Mars. Then Mars Express was launched in 2003. It has been orbiting Mars, observing the surface and the weather. It has discovered water ice at the bottom of the southern ice cap.

Two spacecraft called Mars Exploration Rovers were launched in 2003. Their names are Spirit and Opportunity. When they landed in 2004 they explored the surface and discovered there was definitely water at their landing sites at some time in the past. The Mars Reconnaissance Orbiter was sent to Mars in 2005. It will make maps of Mars to find landing sites for future missions.

▼ An artist's impression of Mars Odyssey

Questions about Mars

There is still a lot to learn about Mars. One day, astronomers hope to find out the answers to questions such as these:

 Are there any active volcanoes on Mars?

 Why are the ice caps on the north and south poles so different from each other?

 Definite evidence of life on Mars has not been found. Could there be living things on Mars in places where no one has looked yet?

 Did water really flow on Mars? If it did, where did it come from, and where did it go? Why was it only flowing for a fairly short time?

 How much water ice is under the ground on Mars?

 Would humans living on Mars be able to use the underground ice for water, and to make oxygen?

▼ One day, there might be humans living and working on Mars.

Mars Fact Summary

Distance from Sun (average)	141,550,000 miles (227,940,000 kilometers)
Diameter (at equator)	4,219 miles (6,794 kilometers)
Mass	0.11 times Earth's mass
Density	3.94 times the density of water
Gravity	0.38 times Earth's gravity
Temperature	(summer) 81 degrees Fahrenheit (27 degrees Celsius), (winter) –207 degrees Fahrenheit (–133 degrees Celsius)
Rotation on axis	24.62 Earth hours
Revolution	686.98 Earth days
Number of moons	2

Web Sites

www.amnh.org/rose/mars
Welcome to Mars!

www.nineplanets.org/
The eight planets—a tour of the solar system

www.enchantedlearning.com
Enchanted Learning Web site—click on "Astronomy"

stardate.org
Stargazing with the University of Texas McDonald Observatory

pds.jpl.nasa.gov/planets/welcome.htm
Images from NASA's planetary exploration program

Glossary

astronomers people who study stars, planets, and other bodies in space

atmosphere a layer of gas around a large body in space

axis an imaginary line through the middle of an object, from top to bottom

core the center, or middle part of a solar system body

craters bowl-shaped hollows in the ground

crust the outside, or layer of a planet

crystals tiny pieces of pure substance

dense heavy for its size

diameter the distance across

equator an imaginary line around the middle of a globe

extinct no longer living or active

gas a substance in which the particles are far apart, not solid or liquid

gravity a force which pulls one body towards another body

hemisphere half of a globe

irregular not evenly shaped

lava hot liquid rock

mantle the middle layer, underneath the crust

mass a measure of how much substance is in something

molten melted into a liquid

moons natural bodies which circle around planets or other bodies

orbit *noun* the path a body takes when it moves around another body; *verb* to travel on a path around another body

planet a large, round body which circles the Sun, and does not share its orbit with other bodies (except its moons)

poles the top and bottom of a globe

revolve travel around another body

rotates spins

space probe an unmanned spacecraft

star a huge ball of glowing gas in space

telescope an instrument for making objects look bigger and more detailed

trans-Neptunian objects small solar system bodies which orbit the Sun farther out than Neptune, on average

volcanoes holes in the ground through which lava flows

Index

Dropping In On...

KENYA

David C. King

A Geography Series

ROURKE BOOK COMPANY, INC.
VERO BEACH, FLORIDA 32964

A Blackbirch Graphics book.
Series Editor: Tanya Lee Stone

Printed in the United States of America.

Library of Congress Cataloging-in-Publication Data

King, David C.
  Kenya / by David C. King.
    p.   cm. — (Dropping in on)
  Includes index.
  ISBN 1-55916-083-7
  1. Kenya—Juvenile literature. I. Title.
II. Series.
  DT433.522.K56   1995
  967.62—dc20   95-10079
                             CIP
                             AC

FIRST FACTS

Kenya
•••••••••••••••

Official Name: Republic of Kenya

Area: 224,960 square miles

Population: 28,241,000

Capital: Nairobi

Largest City: Nairobi (1,600,000)

Highest Elevation:

Mt. Kenya (17,058 feet)

Official Languages: Swahili and

English

Major Religions: Protestant,

Roman Catholic, and Muslim

Money: Shilling

Form of Government: Republic

Flag:

TABLE OF CONTENTS

Our Blue Ball—The Earth

The Earth can be divided into two hemispheres. The word hemisphere means "half a ball"—in this case, the ball is the Earth.

The equator is an imaginary line that runs around the middle of the Earth. It separates the Northern Hemisphere from the Southern Hemisphere. North America— where Canada, the United States, and Mexico are located—is in the Northern Hemisphere.

The Hemispheres

When the North Pole is tilted toward the sun,
the sun's most powerful rays strike the northern
half of the Earth and less sunshine hits the
Southern Hemisphere. That is when people in
the Northern Hemisphere enjoy summer. When

the North Pole is tilted away from the sun, and the
Southern Hemisphere receives the most sunshine,
the seasons reverse. Then winter comes to the
Northern Hemisphere. Seasons in the Northern
Hemisphere and the Southern Hemisphere are
always opposite.

Get Ready for Kenya

Let's take a trip! Climb into your hot-air balloon and we'll drop in on a country on the east coast of Africa. Kenya is slightly smaller than the state of Texas and nearly 27 million people live here. Part of the country is bordered by the Indian Ocean. Kenya is famous for its beautiful scenery and for its wildlife, including elephants, lions, and giraffes.

The equator runs through Kenya. This means that the sun is directly overhead all year, so the climate is usually warm or hot.

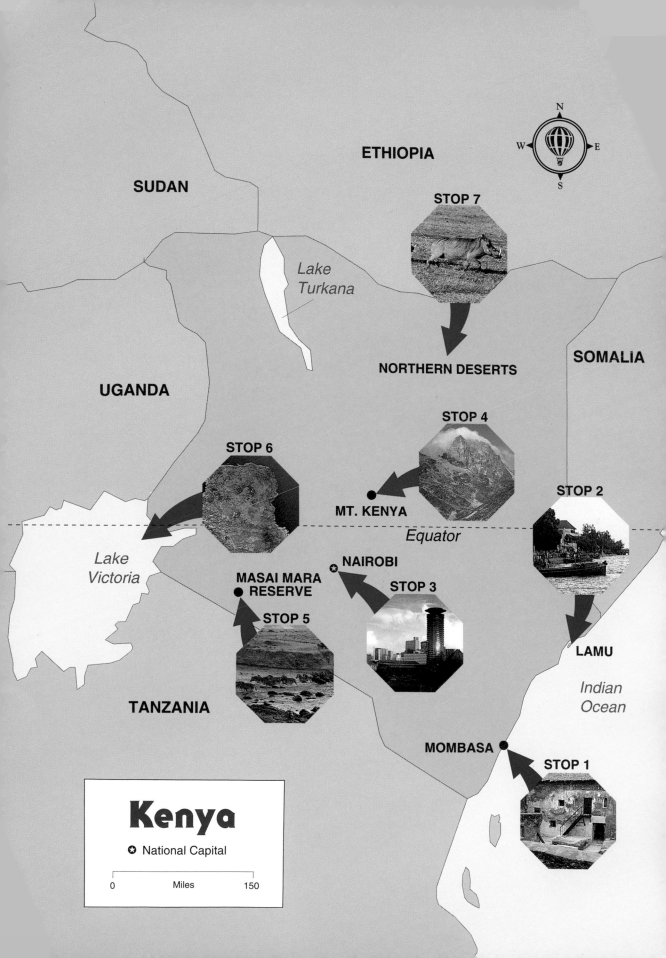

Kenya

ETHIOPIA

SUDAN

SOMALIA

UGANDA

Lake
Turkana

STOP 7

NORTHERN DESERTS

STOP 4

STOP 6

STOP 2

MT. KENYA

Equator

Lake
Victoria

NAIROBI

MASAI MARA
RESERVE

STOP 3

LAMU

Indian
Ocean

STOP 5

TANZANIA

MOMBASA

STOP 1

N
W   E
S

⊛ National Capital

0   Miles   150

Stop 1: Mombasa

Our first stop is the city of Mombasa. Most of the city is built on an island in the Indian Ocean. The island is connected to the mainland by a causeway and 2 bridges. Cars, trucks, and a railroad use the causeway to reach the city.

Mombasa is an old city, first built by Muslim traders more than 1,000 years ago. This is the second-largest city in Kenya, with about 425,000 people. Mombasa is also the major seaport for the country. Products grown on Kenyan farms are shipped by train to Mombasa. Kenya's farmers grow coffee, tea, sugar, cotton, and sisal. Sisal is a plant fiber used to make rope. At the harbor, these goods are loaded onto ocean freighters and then they are shipped to other countries.

At the entrance to the harbor is a huge stone fort built more than 400 years ago. The fort is now a museum where you can learn about the many battles fought there.

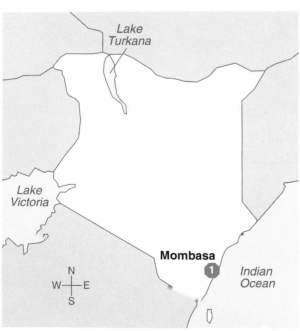

In Mombasa, you can visit an old stone fort that is now a museum.

Most of Mombasa has changed little in the past 100 years. The newer office buildings and homes are on the outskirts or on the mainland. Modern hotels are strung along the coast of the mainland. Vacationers come from as far away as Europe to visit the Indian Ocean beaches near Mombasa.

*Next, we'll travel **northeast** to the island of Lamu.*

Dhows, or fishing boats, are always traveling in and out of Lamu's busy harbor.

Lake Turkana

Lake Victoria

Lamu

Indian Ocean

N
W · E
S

SITAWA

Stop 2: Lamu

Lamu is also an island in the Indian Ocean, and the town of Lamu is the oldest in Kenya. Hundreds of years ago, Lamu was part of a society called Swahili. Swahili is a mixture of African and Muslim customs, ideas, and languages.

Lamu can only be reached by boat or plane. No cars or trucks are allowed on the island. People use donkey carts for transportation. There are very few modern buildings. The narrow, winding dirt streets are lined with walls and houses made of coral blocks, with roofs of tin or coconut palm leaves.

The harbor of Lamu is usually filled with fishing boats called *dhows*. These boats, each with a large sail, were used nearly 2,000 years ago.

The weather on Lamu is usually hot. You might want to stop at a drink house for a fruit shake, made with ice cream and mango, banana, or coconut.

*For our next stop, we'll head **northwest** to the city of Nairobi.*

A young boy uses his donkey cart to transport a bed.

Stop 3: Nairobi

Nairobi is the capital of Kenya and its largest city. A huge valley cuts through the center of Kenya from north to south. It is called the Great Rift Valley. Nairobi is located on highlands above the valley. It has warm days and cool nights.

The building of Nairobi began only 100 years ago. In the downtown area you will see mainly modern buildings.

Nairobi has one of the most unusual parks in the world—Nairobi National Park. From your car or bus, you can see wild animals roaming the grasslands. There are zebras,

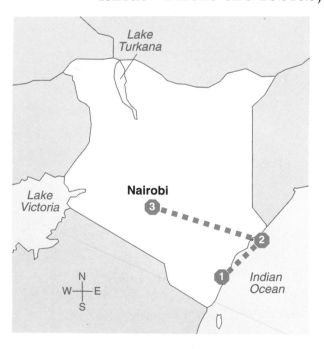

giraffes, lions, and dozens of other animals in the park. In a separate park, you can feed giraffes from a large wooden platform. Near the park entrance is a music and dance center called the Bomas of Kenya. Here you can see the traditional dances of 11 different tribal groups.

Above: A pride of lions rests in the tall grasses. Below: Tall, modern buildings make up the skyline of Nairobi.

Growing Up in Kenya

A little more than half the children in Kenya go to school. Lessons are taught in both Swahili and English. Children study geography, history, math, and science. They go to elementary school until age 11. Then about one out of every seven students goes on to secondary school.

In some village schools, children learn about farming and raising farm animals. Older people come to the school to teach tribal stories, dances, and crafts like wood carving and jewelry making.

The people of Kenya are divided into more than 40 different tribes. Some of the tribes live far from the cities and towns. The people of these tribes live by raising sheep, goats, cattle, and camels. Since they live too far away to attend schools, the children learn the skills they need from their parents.

Boys learn to herd the animals, and they also learn the traditional skills of warriors. Girls are taught to cook, tan leather, weave sisal rope into mats, and make repairs on the family's huts. Many girls also become expert basket weavers or jewelry makers. In many of these distant tribes, a few of the children are chosen to be sent away to school. When they return, these students have new skills and information that can help their tribe.

Schoolchildren from the Masai tribe gather together for a picture.

Now we'll steer our hot-air balloon **northeast** to Mount Kenya.

Clouds brush the top of Mount Kenya, the highest mountain in Kenya.

Stop 4: Mount Kenya

As our hot-air balloon leaves Nairobi, you can see Mount Kenya far in the distance. The mountain towers to a height of 17,058 feet. It is the highest mountain in Kenya.

Even though Mount Kenya is very close to the equator, the peaks are capped with snow and ice. The reason for this is that the air becomes cooler as you climb higher. Thousands of years ago, Mount Kenya was a volcano. Like most of the volcanoes in Kenya, it has not been active for many centuries.

In the foothills below the mountain, we pass tea and coffee plantations. Kenya is one of the world's important growers of tea and coffee. Farther up the mountain slopes, there are smaller farm villages. The Kikuyu and other tribes have farmed here for many years. In tribal religions, Mount Kenya is a sacred place. Still higher up the slopes, the land is covered by bamboo forests.

To the west, you can see Mount Elgon, Kenya's second-highest mountain. Mount Elgon was also once a volcano and has a huge crater almost 4 miles wide.

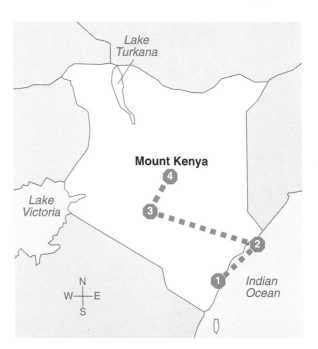

On a tea plantation, tea leaves are carefully picked by workers.

*Next, we'll travel **southwest** to Masai Mara Game Reserve.*

Stop 5: Masai Mara Game Reserve

We are now on the southwestern border of Kenya. The Masai Mara Game Reserve is one of about 40 national parks and game reserves in Kenya. These are special places for the protection of Africa's famous wild animals.

Masai Mara is part of an even larger reserve called the Serengeti Plain, which reaches south into the country of Tanzania. Each year, one of the most amazing migrations on Earth begins in June. About 2 million antelope, called wildebeests, suddenly start traveling north toward the fresher grass of Masai Mara. Soon, other animals join the march.

Thousands of zebras and wildebeests thunder across the Mara River during their yearly migration.

Lake Turkana

Lake Victoria

Masai Mara

Indian Ocean

N
W E
S

Gazelles and 250,000 zebras gallop along. The animals' hoofbeats sound like thunder and the earth shakes.

Lions, leopards, and cheetahs follow along, ready to pounce on stray animals. Wild dogs and hyenas join the hunt, and vultures circle overhead.

From July to November, all of these animals roam through Masai Mara. There are also herds of elephants, giraffes, and buffalo, as well as hippos, crocodiles, storks, ostriches, and flamingos.

One day in November, the wildebeests will suddenly head south. The great Serengeti migration will begin again.

A cheetah guards her young cubs in the Masai Mara Game Reserve.

The Foods of Kenya

For a Swahili breakfast in Kenya, you might try a porridge called *ugali*, or banana pancakes topped with honey.

A Kenyan tribal woman cooks fresh fish for her family over a small fire.

At lunchtime, Kenyans in the cities and towns can enjoy hamburgers or fish and chips (French fries). Dinner usually includes grilled meat or fish, or barbecued beef called *ngombe*. Another favorite is a meat stew made with coconut and coconut milk. With the main dish, you might have *maharagwe*, made with kidney beans, or *matoke*, made with corn and mashed plantains. Plantains are like bananas.

Many of the restaurants are owned by families who migrated to Kenya from India. Indian food is very different from Swahili. You might have an Indian dinner of *tandoori*, made with lamb, chicken, or fish. Many of the dishes are served with rice and a spicy flavoring of curry.

*For our next stop, we'll travel **northwest** to Lake Victoria.*

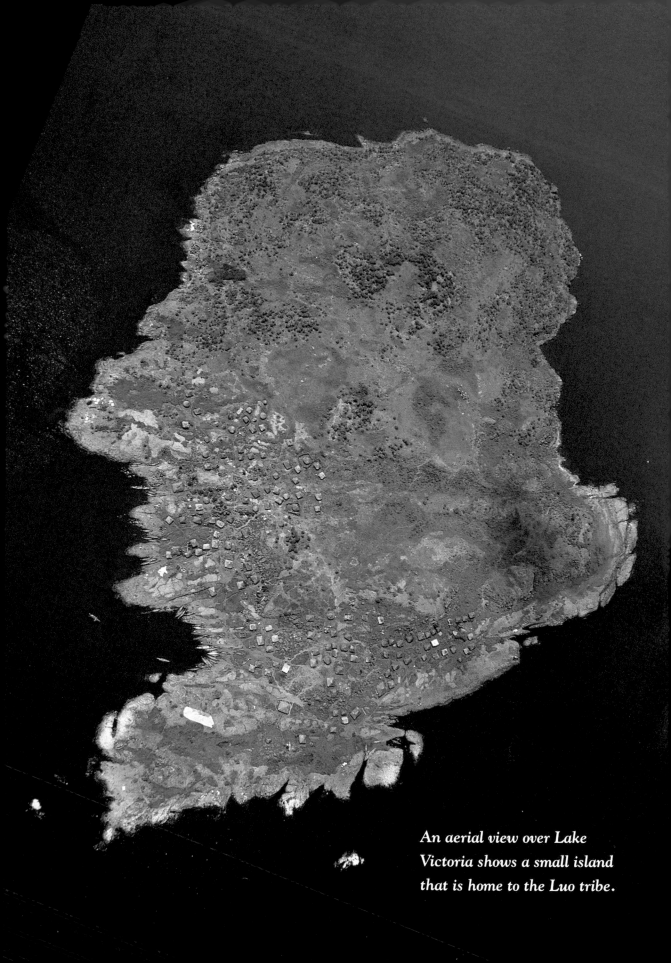

An aerial view over Lake
Victoria shows a small island
that is home to the Luo tribe.

Stop 6: Lake Victoria

As our hot-air balloon soars over western Kenya, we pass over green rolling hills. Below us, you can see farms and plantations growing cotton, sugarcane, tea, and sisal. Some of the houses are round, white-washed huts made of clay with thatch roofs. Other houses are square and have tin roofs.

Farther west, Lake Victoria shimmers in the bright sun. The lake is almost as large as the state of Maine. It is the third-largest lake in the world. Victoria is also the source of the Nile River, the longest river on Earth.

Lake Victoria is quite shallow. Farm and fishing villages dot the shore of the lake. Most of the people living here are members of the Luo tribe. Sailing in small *dhows*, Luo fishermen bring in large catches of fish every day. There are 200 kinds of fish in the lake, but most of the catch will be Nile perch.

For our last stop, we'll head **northeast** into Kenya's northern deserts.

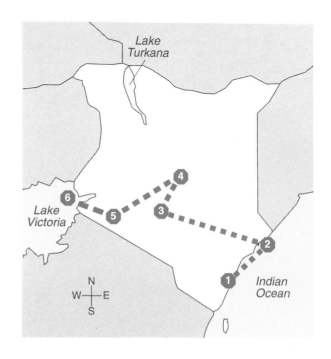

Stop 7: The Northern Deserts

Most of northern Kenya is desert or near-desert. Our hot-air balloon drifts over rugged mountains and the craters of ancient volcanoes that stopped erupting thousands of years ago. The air is hot and dry. In the hills around Lake Turkana, there is a thicker cover of trees and scrub. In this area, you might see elephants, antelopes, warthogs, baboons, and monkeys.

Warthogs are common in the near-deserts of northern Kenya.

A number of tribes live in this sun-baked, wild region. They raise sheep, goats, cattle, and usually some camels, which they use for milk. The tribespeople are nomads who move often in search of grass and water for their herds.

The northern tribes have lived this nomadic life for many generations. They know little about modern life in the cities and towns, but they prefer to live in the old way. Now and then, members of a tribe will visit a town to trade for cloth, tools, or other items. They are skilled in crafts, especially jewelry making. They make beautiful headbands, necklaces, and bracelets out of glass, beads, copper, and even plastic.

Hot-air balloons soar high above Kenya and make large shadows on the flat, dry land.

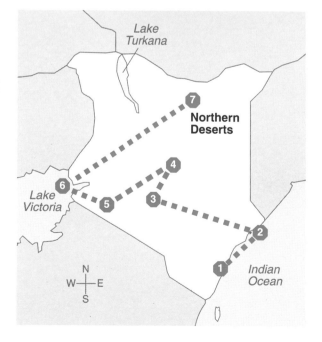

28

A Wildlife Safari

Safari is the Swahili word for "travel," and Kenya is the world's most popular country for wildlife safaris. Every year, more than 1 million people come here to travel on safari through the national parks and reserves.

Most safaris set out from Nairobi or Mombasa. With your safari guide, you travel in a group, riding in a minibus or Land Rover. The trip will last anywhere from 2 days to 2 weeks, or even longer. On

People on safari can photograph animals in natural settings. Here, a safari bus drives past a pair of giraffes.

some safaris, people stay at comfortable lodges in-side the parks. Other travelers prefer to stay in tents and have meals cooked over an open fire.

Twice a day, your guide will take you on a "game drive" to see the animals. With your camera ready, you drive past herds of elephants, and you will probably see giraffes, zebras, baboons, and maybe a pride of lions. The other hunter animals, like leopards and cheetahs, are harder to spot. There will be many different kinds of antelope, such as Thomson's gazelle, wildebeests, impalas, and topi. You might even be lucky enough to spot a rhinoceros. At Masai Mara, you can even take a special safari by hot-air balloon.

In wooded areas you may come across different kinds of monkeys. There are snakes, too, including the cobra, puff adder, and python. At the end of the day, you can go for a swim in the lodge pool. Then, over a hearty dinner of grilled steaks or stew, everyone often talks about the exciting things they saw that day.

Now it's time to steer your hot-air balloon toward home. When you return, you can think back about your great adventure in Kenya.

Index

Acknowledgments and Photo Credits
Cover: ©Eric Horan/Gamma Liaison; pp. 4, 6–7: National Aeronautics and Space
Administration; p. 11: ©C. J. Collins/Photo Researchers, Inc.; p. 12: ©Herlinde Koelbl/Leo
de Wys, Inc.; pp. 13, 14–15, 26: Kenya Tourist Office; p. 17: ©Peter Skinner/Photo
Researchers, Inc.; p. 18: ©Peter Arnold, Inc.; p. 19: ©Richard Saunders/Leo de Wys, Inc.;
pp. 20–21: ©Gregory G. Dimijian, M. D./Photo Researchers, Inc.; p. 22: ©Sven-Olaf
Lindblad/Photo Researchers, Inc.; p. 23: ©Peggy/Yoram Kahana/Peter Arnold, Inc.; pp. 24,
27: ©Y. Arthus-Bertrand/Peter Arnold, Inc.; p. 28: ©W. Hille/Leo de Wys, Inc.
Maps by Blackbirch Graphics, Inc.